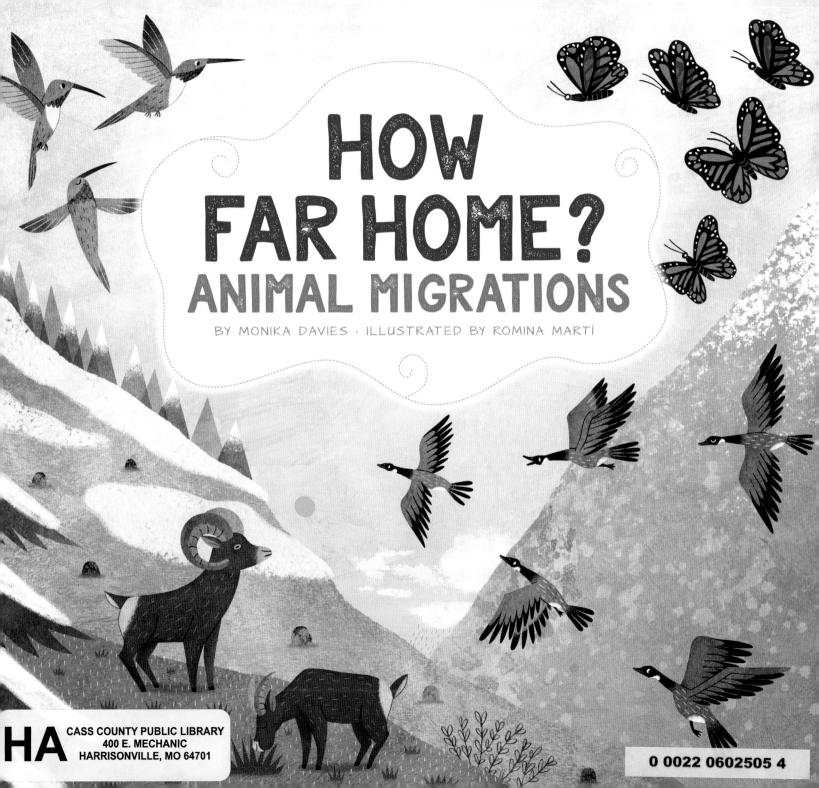

HOW FAR HOME?
ANIMAL MIGRATIONS

BY MONIKA DAVIES · ILLUSTRATED BY ROMINA MARTÍ

Amicus Illustrated and Amicus Ink
are published by Amicus
P.O. Box 1329
Mankato, MN 56002
www.amicuspublishing.us

Library of Congress Cataloging-in-Publication Data
Names: Davies, Monika, author. | Marti, Romina, illustrator.
Title: How far home? : animal migrations / by Monika Davies ; illustrated by Romina Marti.
Other titles: Animal migrations
Description: Mankato, MN : Amicus Illustrated, [2019] | Series: Animals measure up | Audience: K to grade 3. | Includes bibliographical references and index.
Identifiers: LCCN 2017057755 (print) | LCCN 2017058963 (ebook) | ISBN 9781681514673 (pdf) | ISBN 9781681513850 (library binding) | ISBN 9781681523057 (pbk.)
Subjects: LCSH: Animal migration—Juvenile literature. | Animals—Adaptation—Juvenile literature.
Classification: LCC QL754 (ebook) | LCC QL754 .D38 2019 (print) | DDC 591.56/8—dc23
LC record available at https://lccn.loc.gov/2017057755

Editor: Rebecca Glaser
Designer: Kathleen Petelinsek

Printed in the United States of America

HC 10 9 8 7 6 5 4 3 2 1
PB 10 9 8 7 6 5 4 3 2 1

About the Author

When she was young, Monika Davies lived on the Canadian prairies. Every fall, she would watch dozens of Canada geese fly away to their winter home. Now, she also "migrates" to a warmer winter home when the snow begins to fall. Monika graduated from the University of British Columbia with a degree in creative writing. She has written over eighteen books for young readers.

About the Illustrator

Romina Martí is an illustrator who lives and works in Barcelona, Spain, where her ideas come to life for all audiences. She loves to discover and draw all kinds of creatures from around the planet, who then become the main characters for the majority of her work. To learn more, go to: rominamarti.com.

Every year, thousands of animals go on a journey. It is often a trek of many miles. This trip is unique for every species. Some fly. Others climb. Many swim a great distance. But, where are they all going?

Season to season, weather changes. In spring, rain falls. Plants grow. But in winter, the sun sinks lower. The air turns colder.

When the seasons change, many animals travel to a warmer winter home to survive. This journey is called migration. Let's meet a few travelers!

Some migrations are very short! Many snakes live in Shawnee Forest in Illinois. In the summer, these reptiles crowd a wet swamp. But every winter, they slither off, crossing a road to their winter home. The dry cliffs there keep them warm.

Each year, Christmas Island near Australia hosts a great migration. This island is home to red crabs. When the rains begin, the crabs start to move.

0 MILES · 1 · 2

0 KILOMETERS · 1 · 2 · 3

They crawl from the forest to the sea. All of them travel at the same time. When they reach the water, the crabs lay their eggs. This is where their babies are born.

Indonesia

Christmas Island

Bighorn sheep roam high in the Rocky Mountains. They live here in the summer. But when it grows cold, plants up high start to die. The sheep must move homes. They begin a steep climb down. Below, they can find plants to chew. This is how they live through the winter.

Some migrations cover miles and miles. **Honk!** You may have seen—or heard—a Canada goose. These feathered friends migrate every winter.

O MILES   250   500   750

O KM   250   500   750   1,000   1,250

They soar south in flocks, in search of warmer weather. In one day, they can travel up to 1,500 miles (2,414 km). That's the distance from New York City to Austin, Texas!

| | 1,000 | | 1,250 | | 1,500 |
| 1,500 | | 1,750 | 2,000 | | 2,250 | 2,500 |

It is not only birds that fly south in winter. Some insects do too. Every fall, monarch butterflies head south because they can't survive cold winters. Some think a billion monarchs land in Mexico every winter! Here, they mate. They return north in the summer to lay eggs and find food.

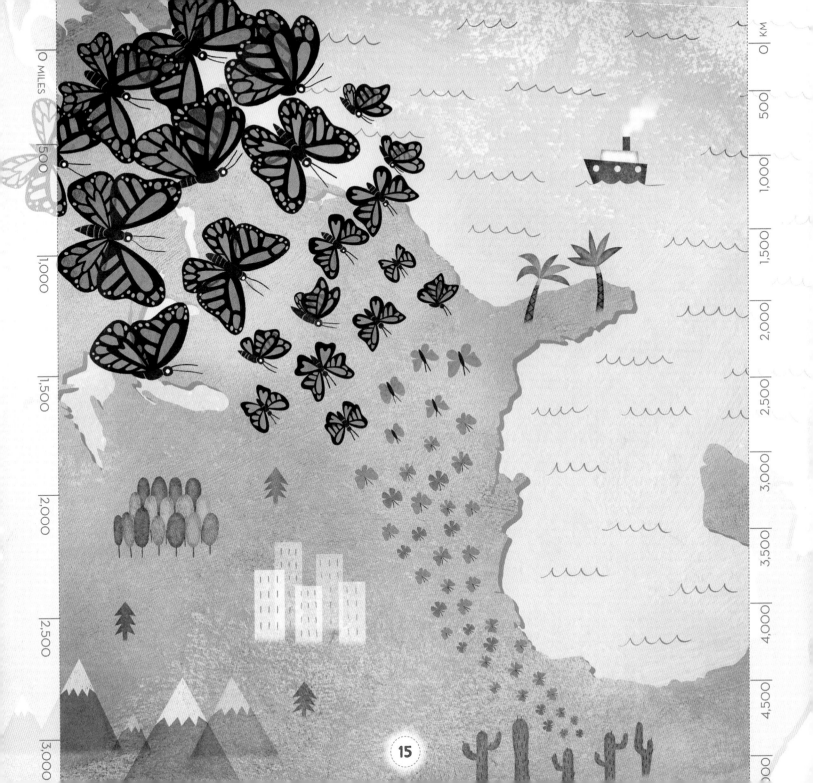

0 KM

500

1,000

1,500

2,000

2,500

3,000

3,500

4,000

4,500

0 MILES

500

1,000

1,500

2,000

2,500

3,000

Even fish change homes! King salmon are born in rivers. In time, they swim to the ocean. But they return home to have babies. To go back, the salmon will swim 2,000 miles (3,219 km). And they must swim upstream!

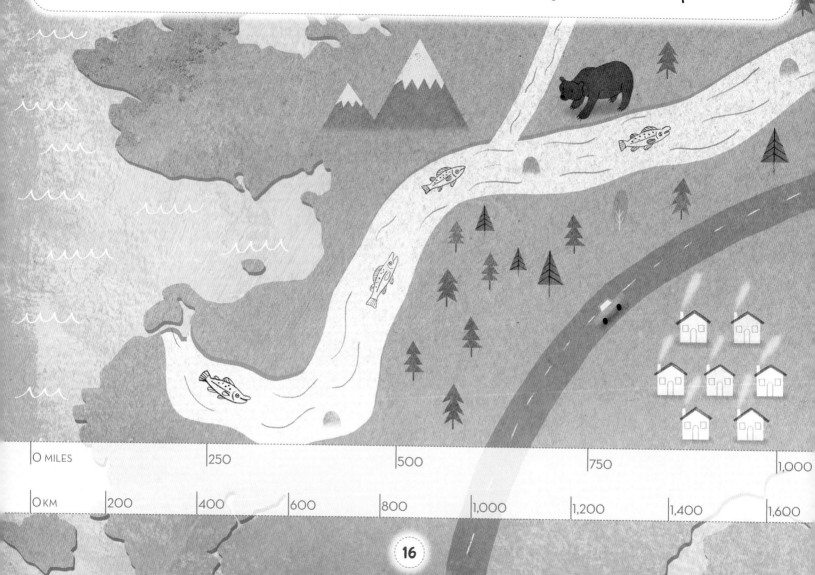

0 MILES	250	500	750	1,000

0 KM	200	400	600	800	1,000	1,200	1,400	1,600

1,250 1,500 1,750 2,000

1,800 2,000 2,200 2,400 2,600 2,800 3,000 3,200

0 MILES
500
1,000
1,500
2,000
2,500
3,000
3,500
4,000

0 KM
1,000
2,000
3,000
4,000
5,000
6,000

Small birds can travel very long distances. The rufous hummingbird has a nectar diet. They need fresh flowers to live. In the winter, they head to sunny spots in Mexico. There, they can find flowers in bloom.

The Arctic tern may be small.
But this sea bird has the world's
longest migration! In summer,
these birds breed near the
Arctic Circle. When they get to
Antarctica, it's summer there too!

MILES
0
1,000
2,000
3,000
4,000
5,000
6,000
7,000
8,000
9,000
10,000

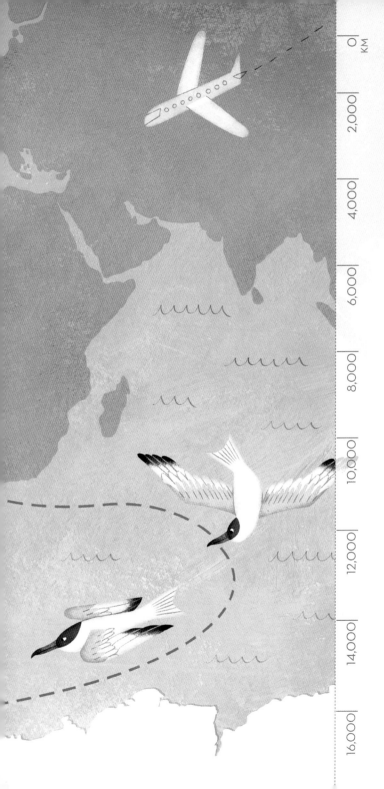

Their S-shaped route to Antarctica and back covers 59,650 miles (96,000 km)! Migration journeys will always be one of nature's wonders.

NORTH AMERICAN MIGRATION ROUTES

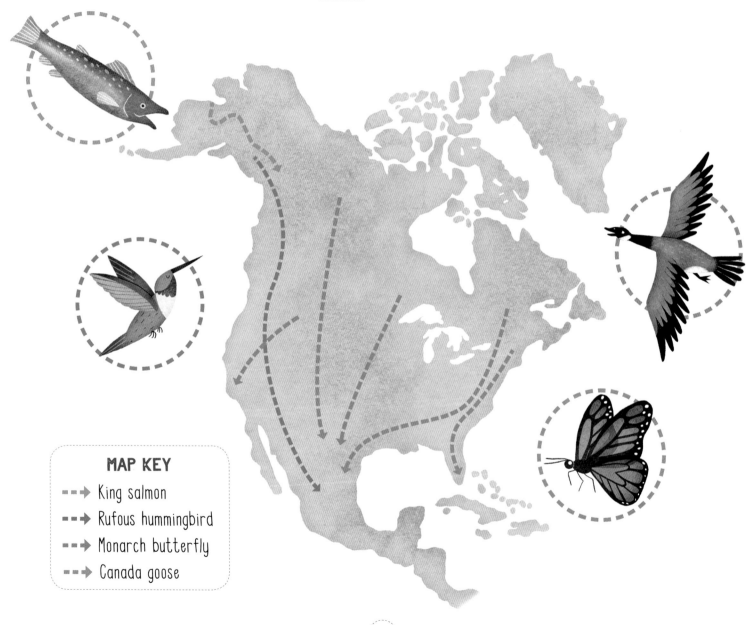

MAP KEY

- - -→ King salmon
- - -→ Rufous hummingbird
- - -→ Monarch butterfly
- - -→ Canada goose

GLOSSARY

flock A group of animals.

insect A bug; a small animal that has six legs and a body formed of three parts and that may have wings.

migration To move from one area to another at different times of the year.

nectar A sweet liquid produced by plants.

reptile An animal that is cold-blooded, that lays eggs, and that has a body covered with scales or hard parts.

species A group of animals or plants that are similar and can produce young animals or plants.

swamp Land that is always wet and often partly covered with water.

READ MORE

Hirsch, Rebecca E. **Thousand-Mile Fliers and Other Amazing Migrators**. Minneapolis: Lerner Publications, 2017.

Norris, Robert. **On the Move: Animal Migration**. North Mankato, MN: Rourke Educational Media, 2016.

Packham, Chris. **Amazing Animal Journeys**. New York: Sterling Children's Books, 2016.

WEBSITES

Animals on the Move – NASA Space Place

https://spaceplace.nasa.gov/migration/en/

Meet many unique animals that migrate to winter homes—who are tracked by NASA satellites!

Bird Migration: The Show – Idaho Public Television

http://idahoptv.org/sciencetrek/topics/bird_migration/

Watch a video of migrating birds and discover why these birds fly to their winter homes!

Migration Route Map – RSPB

https://www.rspb.org.uk/kids-and-schools/kids-and-families/kids/play/migrationmap.aspx

Have a peek at the migration journeys of different animals around the world!

Every effort has been made to ensure that these websites are appropriate for children. However, because of the nature of the Internet, it is impossible to guarantee that these sites will remain active indefinitely or that their contents will not be altered.